£2.00

D1587457

# PET OWNER'S GUIDE TO THE

# Labrador Retriever

## SECOND EDITION

## Diana Beckett

RINGPRESS

# ACKNOWLEDGEMENTS

Thanks to Nancy Quaranto (Zucchero) for help
in providing dogs to photograph.

**Published by Ringpress Books,**
**a division of Interpet Publishing,**
**Vincent Lane, Dorking,**
**Surrey, RH4 3YX, UK.**
Tel: 01306 873822  Fax: 01306 876712
email: sales@interpet.co.uk

SECOND EDITION First published 2003
©2003 Ringpress Books Limited. All rights reserved

## ISBN 1 86054 273 5

Printed and bound in Hong Kong through Printworks International Ltd.

# CONTENTS

# 1 INTRODUCING THE LABRADOR

Many theories have been put forward as to the origins of the Labrador, and it is sometimes difficult to separate fact from fiction.

However, the breed has always attracted thoughtful and diligent breeders, who have kept detailed records, and this has proved to be a tremendous bonus in the development of the Labrador.

The history of the breed can be traced back to Newfoundland, a bleak, inhospitable region of

Canada, discovered by John Cabot in the 15th century, although archaeological discoveries have located Viking settlements dating back to at least AD 1000.

## EARLY ANCESTORS

When John Cabot set foot on Newfoundland, it was deserted. The Vikings had left, native Americans had been and gone, and Eskimos, a race well known for working with dogs, had also left the region. No traces of dogs were found, but, in later years, archaeologists found remains of a large dog, which could have been the forerunner of the Newfoundland dog, and a companion of the early native American settlers.

# THE FISHERMAN'S DOG

John Cabot was quick to discover the fishing potential of Newfoundland, and soon the English fishing fleet was at work off the coasts. This was around 1450-1458.

The fleet owners were hard taskmasters, and they were ever mindful of competition. Fishermen were forbidden to settle on the islands, in case they got ideas of setting up their own industry.

But settle they did, in spite of a law forbidding settlement within six miles of the coast.

It was a hard, rough life, and the fishermen, who were mostly from Devon and Dorset, were a tough, hard-bitten lot. They were illiterate to a man, but wise in all manner of country pursuits, including the capture of game for the pot.

They probably had dogs at home who retrieved birds or rabbits from right under the gamekeepers' noses, and these four-legged partners in crime were sorely missed when it came to finding food in a foreign land.

*Fisherman's friend: The Labrador is famous for its willingness to work in water.*

## ENGLISH OR CANADIAN?

Now comes the all-important question: did they take their dogs on the boats with them from England, or did they find a dog that could be trained as a helpmate in this new country?

It is documented that the Devon and Dorset fishermen in those days fished from off the Newfoundland coat in a boat known as the dory – an open boat, rowed with heavy sweeps or oars. They invariably had a dog on board, which was smaller than a Newfoundland, with a shorter, denser coat, and a willingness to enter the icy waters to retrieve fish that had escaped from the nets.

### Water Babies

I believe the dogs who swam out to the nets must have been the larger 'Newfoundland' type dog. The smaller type had many of the same attributes, namely a willingness to work in water, and a coat that shed water quickly and was so dense that the dog could withstand the icy conditions.

These were the two types of dogs that assisted the early settlers in the 16th century.

By the early 1800s, both types were found in the St. John's area

*The special Labrador coat allowed dogs to work in cold, wet conditions.*

of Newfoundland. One, a heavy-coated, large, black animal, was used not only for swimming out with the nets, but also as a draught dog, pulling sleds of dried fish. The other, a smaller, dense-coated dog, was good at retrieving on land and water. We can only speculate as to whether the smaller dog came over from England. It could have been a cross from the English St. Hubert Hound.

## THE SHOOTING COMPANION

The continuous trade between Newfoundland and England meant the St. John's Dog, with a reputation as a retriever second to none, was soon noticed by English sportsmen. The second Earl of Malmesbury lived near Poole in Dorset, which was one of the principal ports in the Newfoundland fishing trade. Lord Malmesbury and Colonel Peter Hawker bought several dogs from the fishermen. In fact, it was Colonel Hawker, who, around 1812, gave names to the two types of dog. The larger dog became known as the Newfoundland, and the smaller dog was known as the Lesser Newfoundland, the Labrador, or the St. John's Dog.

Colonel Hawker wrote a book in 1814 called *Instruction To Young Sportsmen*, in which he described the Labrador as "by far the best dog for every kind of shooting".

## POPULARITY BOOST

It was not long before the Labrador's reputation became more widespread, and the Duke of Buccleuch, Lord Home, and the Hon. Arthur Holland-Hibbert (later to become Lord Knutsford) joined the band of Labrador owners. They were an informed group of fanciers, and, fortunately for us, they bred true to type, and kept records of their dogs' pedigrees.

### INFLUENTIAL DOGS

Buccleuch Avon was one of the earliest important dogs, and he was probably the ancestor of all black Labradors. Avon, who was sired by Malmesbury Tramp out of a bitch called June, was bred by Lord Malmesbury in 1885. He was given to the Duke of Buccleuch along with two Labradors, namely Ned and Nell. Avon was reported to have been a lovely dog, with a splendid head and the kindest of expressions. It has been stated that his birth was the most important date in the history of the Labrador. The other famous dog of this early time was Nell, owned by the 11th Earl of Howes. Photographs show she had a good head with a lovely, kind expression. She had four white feet, but, through careful breeding, this fault was eliminated, and we now have the whole-coloured dog known today as the Labrador Retriever.

The Hon. Arthur Holland-Hibbert was particularly noted for producing good, sound dogs, and his strain was given the kennel name of Munden. In fact, it was a dog called Munden Single who, in 1904, became the first Labrador to run in a Field Trial. In the same year, Labradors were listed as a separate breed by the UK Kennel Club, and all seven registered were from the Munden kennel.

## Versatile All-rounder

Since those early days, the Labrador Retriever has excelled in many roles. It remains a gundog *par excellence*; it is among the most popular breeds to be used as guide dogs for the blind, and its tremendous sense of smell makes it ideal as a sniffer dog.

Most important of all, the Labrador's outstanding temperament, marked by his willingness to please, makes the breed one of the world's most popular and best-loved family companions.

*The temperament of the Labrador is second to none.*

11

# 2 CHOOSING A PUPPY

Now that you have decided to own a dog, and you have chosen the Labrador Retriever as the breed you want, it is worthwhile spending a little time on choosing the right puppy.

Remember, this is to be your companion and your family's companion for, hopefully, the next 10 years or more.

## CHILD'S PLAY

If you have a young family, or you plan to have children, it is a good idea to have a puppy grow up with them, providing you give the pup the attention he deserves – or that he has got used to prior to the advent of a baby.

As children grow older and more mobile, do not allow them to poke and pull at a puppy or at an older dog. Children must learn to respect animals. I always said to my children: "If you torment the dogs and they bite you, it will be you I shall punish". I now hear my children giving the same lesson to their children, and I believe it is essential for all dog owners with children to establish a mutual understanding.

Generally, Labradors seem to have a great affinity with children. Toddlers are the right size to be used as pillows on the floor, or as constant suppliers of food. As the children get older, they become playmates – someone who will throw a ball or take the dog on exciting walks.

There are drawbacks to taking on a Labrador puppy that you should be aware of:

- The puppy will miss his mother and brothers and sisters, and the first few nights may be sleepless, for all concerned.
- The pup will need to be house-trained.
- There will also be the teething stage when the pup chews everything in sight, including the furniture.

*Family dog: The Labrador fits in with adults and children alike.*

# THE OLDER DOG

If you are going to be away during the day for long periods of time, such as being out at work, then it may be a better idea to acquire an older dog, who has already been taught some manners. This also applies if you are older, and you do not want to take the chance of being tripped up or knocked down by a boisterous pup.

## Older and Wiser

Many breeders have older kennel dogs that they would like to put into a home where they can become a much-loved family pet, occupying the number-one spot on the hearth-rug, instead of living in a kennel for the rest of their lives.

There are many reasons why older dogs become available from breeders. It could be that the dog has been retained as a potential show dog, only to find that he is not up to show standard, or it may be that the dog dislikes showing. There are also bitches who have grown too old to be bred from, or stud dogs who are no longer to be used for this purpose.

Kennel dogs have usually been lead- and car-trained, and, as most of them have been self-taught to be clean in their kennels, they adapt very quickly to being clean in a house.

The other way to obtain an older dog is through a Labrador Retriever rescue scheme (your kennel club or breed club secretary will have details).

# MALE OR FEMALE?

It is a matter of personal choice whether you want a dog or a bitch. However, do not let people tell you that males are not so loving or so easy to train as females. I find just the opposite; my bitches tend to be far more independent.

The other thing in a dog's favour is that you do not have to cope with seasons. A bitch comes into season roughly every six months, and this will happen throughout her life, unless you have her spayed, which is an added expense to consider.

Some new owners fear that a male will develop a wanderlust, but, in fact, Labradors are not usually great wanderers.

However, as a responsible owner, you must ensure that your dog – male or female – is not allowed to stray away from your home.

The adult male is a little larger and heavier than the female, but he can be just as sweet-tempered, loving and faithful as any bitch. I must admit that I prefer males to females. I like that extra bit of verve and cheekiness that seem to exude from them. However, this is purely a matter of personal choice, and everyone has their own feelings on the subject.

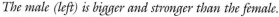

*The male (left) is bigger and stronger than the female.*

*Each colour has its own band of enthusiasts.*

# COLOUR

Coat colour is another matter of personal preference. Labradors can be black, yellow or chocolate coloured, and the yellow can range from light cream to red-fox. Regardless of colour, they are all one breed, with the same height, weight, coat texture, temperament and intelligence.

There is no escape when it comes to moulting; all three varieties shed their coats, so it is a matter of deciding which colour hairs show up on your carpets! We keep both black and yellow, as I prefer blacks, and my husband has always preferred yellows.

If you are planning to breed, I would not recommend starting with a chocolate, unless you can call on specialised advice from your puppy's breeder. The coat and pigment (skin colour) are not the easiest to keep true unless you know what you are doing. You also have to hope that the sun does not shine all the time, as it is liable to play havoc with the coat colouring.

If you want to use your Labrador as a gundog, your local terrain can also play an important part in your choice of colour. If you are surrounded by cornfields, a black dog can really stand out in the stubble, whereas a yellow blends in beautifully.

Likewise, a black blends in

better than a pale yellow on moorland.

I have found that if you lose a much-loved Labrador, either through old age or any other reason, it is sometimes easier to replace that dog with a puppy of the opposite sex, or with a different coloured pup.

However, every dog has his own personality, so a new dog really is a new dog, regardless of sex or colour. Whether he is black, yellow or chocolate, dog or bitch, whether he is an only dog or one of a crowd – if he is a Labrador, you are certain to enjoy him!

*Taking on a dog is a big commitment.*

## FINDING A BREEDER

When you have decided whether you want a puppy or an older animal, a dog or a bitch, and which colour you prefer, the next step is to find a breeder. Always buy from a recognised breeder. Your national kennel club can give you a list of breeders in your area, or can put you in contact with a breed club secretary.

There is little point in looking at a litter prior to five weeks of age. The puppies need to be up on their feet and running around, and, by this time, they will have developed a little bit of personality.

- If possible, see both the sire and the dam of the puppy you are considering, but, as most breeders travel to a stud dog, you will usually only find the dam at the breeder's home or kennel.

# ASSESSING THE PUPPIES

- When you view a litter, the puppies should be housed in a clean, draught-proof area with enough room to move in, and the pups should look as if they are enjoying life. Cleanliness, light and space show that the breeder knows what he or she is doing.
- The puppies should smell 'puppyish'. It is a smell that is hard to describe, but it is clean and wholesome, and makes you want to pick up the pup and cuddle him.
- The puppies should be clean and appear healthy, with bright eyes and wagging tails.
- It is nice to see the puppies come running up to you, but do not completely dismiss the pup that holds his ground and looks at

*Sometimes a puppy will seem to choose you!*

you – this could be the 'thinker' of the litter, the one who is going to weigh up everything.

- The pup to avoid, unless you are prepared to spend extra time and effort working on him, is the one that runs away looking frightened. A Labrador Retriever should have a sound, outgoing character, and a reserved dog is not the one for a noisy family.

*Watch the pups at play to get an idea of their individual characters.*

## WELCOME VISITOR

When you have picked out your puppy, go back as many times as is convenient for both you and the breeder, to see your pup. If, for any reason, you cannot go back too often, do not worry that you might be given the wrong one. All breeders have their own method of marking a pup that is sold. The breeder will give you a date to go to pick up your little treasure, and that is usually at about eight weeks old.

**Before you go to collect your puppy, you will need to purchase a few items of equipment:**
- **Bed/indoor crate**
- **Collar and lead**
- **Grooming equipment**
- **Safe, durable toys**
- **Food (see page 20).**

# FOOD FOR THOUGHT

As far as food is concerned, be guided by your puppy's breeder, who will usually give you a diet sheet that takes you through the first six months of life. Some breeders provide food to take the puppy through the first couple of days, otherwise make sure you know what the breeder has been feeding, so that you can buy some ready for the new arrival.

You may want to change the diet at a later date, but it is important that you stick to the food your puppy is used to for the first few weeks at least, and then gradually change over, introducing the new food a little at a time. The pup is facing a complete change in his environment, and, if you change his feeding habits as well, you could put him through a lot of needless stress.

## THE BIG DAY

When you go to collect your Lab, take along a driver, so you can reassure the pup. Before you take him home, ask the breeder about the dog's worming programme, to determine when the next treatment is due. You will also need to find out if the puppy has received any inoculations. The breeder should also provide you with a copy of your puppy's pedigree and the paperwork you will need in order to register him with your national kennel club.

*A crate is ideal if you bring your puppy home by car.*

# HOME AT LAST

Try to make the transition as trouble-free as possible for your puppy. Your home represents an entire new way of life. A puppy is leaving his mother and littermates, and has to cope with a whole series of new experiences. If you are buying an older dog, he may have lived in a kennel all his life and will feel unsure of his new surroundings.

In both situations, the dog has to become confident with you and learn your habits.

## Life Changes

He also has to adjust in many other ways: the time you get up in the morning, the time you go to bed, the time he is fed, and he may have to get used to being exercised on a lead.

If you acquire an older dog, call him by the name he is used to. Do not be jealous if you meet up with the former owners and your dog makes a big fuss of them. After all, the previous owner probably loved him as much as

*Your pup will feel lost to begin with, so give him time to adjust to his new home.*

you do now. If you give the dog understanding and let him gain his confidence with you, it will work out. You will learn from one another.

21

# 3 BEST OF CARE

Now that you have collected your puppy, who is, hopefully, a lively, well-fed little bundle, you will want to know how to keep him that way.

This is not as daunting as it sounds, as long as you follow a few simple guidelines.

## FEEDING

If you have bought from a responsible breeder, you will have been supplied with a diet sheet. This will guide you for the first few months.

Do not worry if your puppy goes off his food for the first two or three days. Remember, this is probably the first time that the puppy has been on his own, and he does not have the stimulation of competing for food with his brothers and sisters. Do not despair. If your puppy does not eat his food within 10 minutes, just pick up the bowl and wait until the next mealtime.

A puppy will not deliberately starve himself, and, if he is more hungry when you offer the next meal, he is more likely to forget his nerves and settle down to his food! It may be advisable to reduce the amount you offer at each mealtime until the pup finds his feet and eats all he is given at the correct time.

## Familiar Food

It is advisable to try to keep the puppy on the same food that the breeder has been using. A change of lifestyle and surroundings are enough for a pup to cope with without having to deal with a new type of food. However, any problems with feeding are likely to be short-lived, as Labradors as a

*Most Labrador puppies are always hungry.*

breed are very 'good doers' and they very seldom need to be coaxed to eat – often the reverse is true!

Methods of rearing puppies and

## COLD COMFORT

**Remember, if you are serving food from the refrigerator, take it out a little while before you serve it, so that it can reach room temperature.**

young stock vary from breeder to breeder. We have all tried new ways; some have been converted and some still prefer the old ways. I must admit that I have become a convert, and, after the first one to two weeks of giving the puppies their first solid feeds, I go on to feeding one of the 'all-in-one' complete diets. However, I still feed two milk feeds, and I also occasionally add an egg or some cheese. This works for me, and my pups seem to be quite happy and healthy. The new owners also seem to find that the puppies thrive on this diet.

Obviously, the method you choose is a matter of personal choice, and below is listed the 'traditional' diet, and the 'modern' diet, both of which are suitable for a puppy at eight weeks of age. However, please do as your breeder recommends for the first week or two, and then, if you decide that you want to change, do it slowly, gradually introducing your puppy to the new type of food over a few days.

# TRADITIONAL DIET

- Breakfast (8am): Porridge made with warm milk and baby cereal, or warm milk with brown bread (a fruit-bowl full). A raw egg can be mixed with this about twice a week. Vitamin supplements can be mixed with this feed.
- Lunch (noon): 6 to 8 oz of raw, chopped beef, plus 2 to 3 oz of soaked puppy meal. This must be a good-quality wholemeal biscuit.
- Snack (3pm): Same amount as for breakfast, but use milk and baby rusks, or make a baked egg custard, or give half a can of rice pudding.
- Supper (6pm): Same as for lunch.
- Last thing at night: Small biscuit to go to bed with.

Looking at this diet sheet, I wonder when I ever found time to do anything else when I had a litter of puppies to rear. This is one of the reasons why I changed to the following diet.

*Choosing the correct diet is all-important when your puppy is growing.*

## MODERN DIET

- Breakfast (8am): 4 to 6 oz of pre-soaked, 'all-in-one' feed, or as recommended on the bag of feed. Make sure you choose a good-quality brand of complete diet – be guided by your pup's breeder.
- Lunch (noon): Powdered goat's milk or fresh goat's milk, or semi-skimmed cow's milk heated and added to porridge. Feed a fruit-bowl full, using a quarter to a half-pint of milk.
- Tea (4pm): Repeat the meal served at breakfast-time.
- Supper (6-7pm): Same as lunch. Do not feed this after 7pm, as it could hinder your pup's house-training.
- Last thing at night: Small biscuit to go to bed with.

Complete diets are quick and easy to feed, and you can rest assured they contain all the nutrients a growing Labrador needs. As your dog matures, he can be switched to an adult version of the diet.

## REDUCING FEEDS

As your puppy grows older, you should start reducing the number of feeds, and increasing the quantity. The first to go are the milk feeds, and I recommend that, at 12 weeks, you cut out the afternoon snack if you are feeding the traditional diet (the 6pm feed on the modern diet – see page 24), and give a little more at the two meat-and-biscuit or all-in-one feeds.

Depending on how your puppy is maturing, cut out the other milk feed at six to eight months, and give just two feeds of meat and meal or two feeds of all-in-one per day. At nine months, your young dog will only need one meal a day, and a biscuit to go to bed with. In terms of quantity, this should be 1.5 lbs of all-in-one, or 1 lb of meat and 8 to 12 oz of biscuit meal a day.

The time of day you choose to feed your dog should be the time that is going to work out the most convenient for you. If you decide on first thing in the morning, then start to take away the afternoon feed and add to the morning feed, and likewise, in reverse, if you decide to feed in the evening.

*At around six months of age, a Labrador will need two meals a day.*

# WORMING

When you collect your puppy from the breeder, you should be given details of the worming programme that has been followed, and you will need to know when the next treatment is due. At this age, pups suffer mainly from roundworms, and they are easily treated. Some breeders start to worm at four weeks of age, and then again at two-weekly intervals. Other breeders worm at five and seven weeks, or six to eight weeks.

*All dogs must be treated for worms.*

It is advisable to give your puppy a chance to settle down in his new home and learn to cope with his new feeding schedule and other routines before you worm again, and 12 weeks is an ideal time. If your vet sees your pup prior to this age, you can seek advice on a worming routine and you can use the medication your vet recommends. All are very easy to administer, and it is very rare for a puppy to suffer from any side effects following medication.

It is important to weigh your pup before worming, and then

27

give the dose as directed. Most modern remedies dissolve the worms before they are expelled, but you should always check the stools for the 24-hour period after worming, and, if worms are passed, pick up immediately and burn or dispose of them safely. Make sure you wash your hands afterwards.

Worming is essential to your puppy's welfare. A puppy that is infested with worms cannot get the full benefit from his food, and may develop a nasty, dry cough, bad breath, and a dull, dry coat. After you have wormed at 12 weeks, worming should be repeated every three or four months throughout your dog's life (in most countries) – your vet will provide you with details.

## INOCULATIONS

Most vets recommend that puppies start their inoculations at 12 weeks of age, but there are a few who like to start them earlier. This may depend on the incidence of diseases in a particular locality, so telephone your vet to find out the local policy, and you can also make an appointment for the first inoculation. Prior to this, make sure that you keep your pup away from places frequented by other dogs. In fact, your puppy should

*The timing of vaccinations may vary.*

not leave the safety of your garden or yard until after the inoculation programme has been completed.

When you go for the first inoculation, carry your pup and do not put him down in the surgery. The main diseases that are covered are distemper, hepatitis, leptospirosis, parvovirus, and, in some countries, rabies. Usually, two injections are given two weeks apart. They will protect your puppy for 12 months. From then onwards, your dog must have an annual booster.

Some vets will recommend that you have your dog inoculated against kennel cough at a later stage.

This is well worth doing, not only if you intend to send your dog to a boarding kennel at any time, but also because this disease is very contagious and it can be

*You may decide to inoculate against kennel cough.*

picked up just by mixing with other dogs in the park or at a dog show.

## KEEP A RECORD

Remember to keep the inoculation card, which will be issued by your vet, in a safe place. This will give you all the dates and details of inoculation, and all reputable boarding kennels will only take dogs with a current inoculation record.

# EXERCISE

A working dog at heart, the Labrador loves to be kept active – physically and mentally – and it is your job to ensure he doesn't get bored.

However, it is important not to over-exercise a growing puppy, as long-term skeletal damage can be done. Strenuous activities, such as climbing the stairs, leaping in and out of the car, and jumping on and off furniture, should be forbidden.

Initially, play in the garden is all that is required; building up to more formal lead-exercise very slowly. Once your Lab is fully mature (at around 12 months), however, the sky's the limit.

Most adult dogs will need a minimum of two half-hour walks a day – but the quality of the walk is far more important than the length of it.

Vary your walks so your dog doesn't become bored with the same surroundings every day. If he encounters new sights, smells and sounds, he will be far more mentally stimulated – and it's more fun for the dog walker too! Find new routes and play games, such as fetch or hide-and-seek, during the walk – anything that will spice up the walk. Labs love water, and this can be incorporated into his exercise regime – just make sure you have lots of towels in the car!

Let your older Lab dictate his exercise requirements. Labs love people and will try their hardest to keep up with their owners –

sometimes to the detriment of their own health. Three or four short walks a day will help to keep your veteran alert without wearing him out.

Again, swimming is excellent for oldies – providing exercise without stressing the joints. However, cold water can play havoc with bones and joints, so ensure he is dried thoroughly after a dip, and perhaps consider taking him to a heated canine hydrotherapy pool.

*Labradors need mental – as well as physical – stimulation.*

# BED TIME!

A dog bed is an important item of equipment, but there are a number of points to consider before you rush into an expensive purchase.

- Wicker: Looks attractive, but few puppies can resist chewing this type of bed. You will be surprised how quickly wicker unravels when chewed, and you will be surprised at how much wicker there is in a basket when it has all unravelled!

*There is a wide variety of dog beds to choose from.*

- Cardboard box: A large cardboard box is a good choice for your pup's first bed. Make sure there are no metal pins in it, and you can cut down the front so that the pup can get in and out easily.
- Plastic: You could buy a rigid plastic bed. These are easy to clean and can be lined with cosy bedding.
- Fabric: Soft and comfortable, this type of bed is usually made of synthetic material and is machine-washable.

## CHEW IT OVER

Make sure that there are no electric wires near the pup's bed, as this is just the sort of thing a puppy likes to try out his teeth on – and the results could be disastrous.

# BEDDING

Most puppies are naturally clean in their bed, so you can put a blanket or towel in the bottom for comfort. Some pups will not be so obliging; in which case, a good layer of newspapers in the bottom will have to suffice for a while. Your yellow puppy may look a little grubby, as the print often rubs off from the newspapers, but it will not do any harm. If you want to avoid this, you can use shredded paper for bedding.

However, you would be advised to wait a while before you give your puppy a pet duvet. If your puppy chews an old blanket, it is not so hard on the pocket; it is easier to clean up the mess, and it is not so harmful if any pieces are swallowed.

I find that fleecy, polyester bedding strips are ideal. They are warm and comfortable for the dog, they can be machine-washed, and they are difficult to chew.

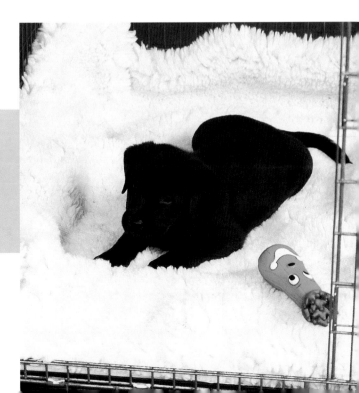

*A pup should feel safe and secure in his sleeping quarters.*

# DROP-OFF POINT

You must also decide where your puppy is
going to sleep, and this is a matter of personal
choice. However, you must ensure that the bed is located
somewhere free of draughts and out of the main thoroughfare,
so that the dog can rest in warmth and comfort. If you choose
a room that has a washable floor with no carpets, such as the kitchen
or utility room, it will make life easier. You must be prepared for a few
'mistakes' to start with, and a mop and bucket is so much easier to use than
a shampoo machine! When your dog is adult, you can buy whatever type
of bed you desire – with a best duvet or blanket in the bottom – and, of
course, you can put it in the sitting room on your best carpet, or
even beside your bed. Be warned, though, your Labrador may start
off in the basket, but, at some time in the early hours, the
temptation to climb on to your bed may become too much,
and an 80-lb Labrador makes a poor bedfellow!

## GREAT CRATES

A crate is the most expensive item of dog equipment, but many owners find it is an invaluable investment. The crate can be set up at home, it can be used in the car, or you can use it as a portable kennel if you are staying away from home.

It is important to train your pup to love his crate. To begin with, make it look as attractive as possible, lining it with cosy bedding, and maybe putting a toy in there, providing it is 100 per cent safe.

The next step is to tempt your pup to go into his crate. You can do this by luring him in with a treat or with his food bowl. Leave the door open, and stroke your pup, telling him what a good boy he is. You can then shut the door, but stay in the same room.

Release your pup after a few minutes, and try again a little later. It is a good idea to choose a time when your pup is tired so he will be more likely to settle.

Gradually build up the amount

of time the pup spends in his crate, and he will soon come to look on it as his own special den.

Remember the following points:

- Never leave your pup in his crate for longer than two hours (unless you are leaving him over night).
- Never use the crate as a means of punishment. It should only be used at times when you cannot supervise your pup, or if you are going out for a short period.

## GROOMING

The Labrador is a short-coated breed, and so does not require a great deal of grooming. All you will need are the basic tools, such as a good brush and a comb, and a weekly grooming session will be sufficient to keep your dog in good condition.

A healthy dog will have a good, glossy coat, and most Labradors love to be brushed. This also helps to bring the new coat back in a little faster when your dog is shedding.

Regular grooming allows you to check the coat for parasites (see Chapter Six), and any cuts, lumps or bumps that may need veterinary attention.

*Accustom your puppy to having his coat brushed.*

### SCRUB UP!

If your dog rolls in something horrible, or if he is losing his coat, a bath with a good-quality medicated dog shampoo will help to get rid of the dirt and also the loose hairs. Do make sure that the suds are rinsed thoroughly afterwards, and test the temperature of the water before wetting your dog. A rub-down with a towel, and then a brush and a comb, and your dog is as good as new.

## Ears

At the weekly grooming session, check your dog's ears. If they are dirty, buy some ear cleaner and use as directed, removing any dirt from the outer part of the ear with cotton wool (cotton). Do not use cotton buds or probe too deeply into the ear.

## Nails

Your dog's nails should be kept short. Regular road-walking should keep them in trim, but, if they grow too long, you will need to snip off the points with a pair of nail-clippers.

Great care should be taken to avoid the 'quick' – the nerves and blood supply of the nails. If you are in any doubt how to trim the nails properly, ask your vet to show you.

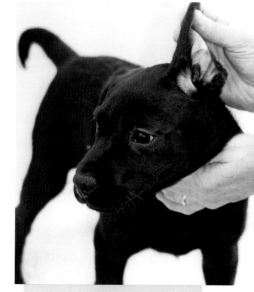

*Above: The ears should be clean and fresh-smelling.*

*Below: Routine nail-trimming may be necessary.*

# 4

## EARLY LEARNING

Everyone wants to own a well-behaved, obedient dog that they can take anywhere and that will not be a nuisance to anyone.

Like all things that are worth achieving, this takes some hard work, but, as a responsible dog owner, you should be prepared to take on the commitment of training your Labrador to become a well-mannered, sociable individual.

This is not only desirable from the dog's point of view – it will make a big difference to your life, too.

## HOUSE-TRAINING

This is the first important lesson that you will want to teach your puppy. Being a highly intelligent breed, Labrador Retrievers are usually quick to catch on, once they know what is expected. In all training, it is important to be consistent, and this is particularly the case with house-training.

● As soon as you have fed your

pup, take him out to the same area and give a command, such as "Be quick" or "Be clean", making sure you always use the same command.

- As soon as your puppy does what is required, give plenty of praise.
- You must be prepared to wait until you get the desired result – the puppy will not learn

anything if you let him out in the garden on his own.

- Do not leave it too long between visits outside. You will be surprised at how often a pup needs to go. The basic rule is to take a puppy out immediately after feeding, every time he wakes up from a rest, after play and excitement, and every two hours during the day.

## PUPPY TRAINING

Puppies are like children, and both should be properly brought up so that they are well behaved and a pleasure to have around. The golden rule is to start as you mean to go on. When you say "No", you must mean it. A puppy must understand what is required, and so you must praise him when he is good, and ignore him when he is naughty.

A puppy has a lot to learn in the first few months of his life. He has to adapt to his new family and his new home, as well as to many new experiences outside the home.

This vital period of socialisation

*Teach your Labrador the house rules – and stick to them.*

is the key to having a well-behaved, well-adapted dog. If you give your puppy time at this stage, you will find it pays dividends when you get down to more serious training.

Although you cannot venture far afield until your puppy has completed his inoculation programme, you can still make progress.

The first step is to build up a bond with your puppy.

If your pup learns to trust you, he will be reassured by your presence when he is confronted by strange things, which he might find alarming.

*Build up trust so your pup will feel confident when it is time to take him out.*

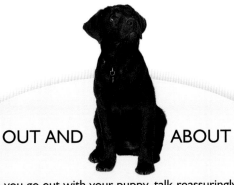

## OUT AND ABOUT

The first time you go out with your puppy, talk reassuringly to him all the time. This keeps your puppy's attention on you, and you will be able to coax him along when he confronts the hustle and bustle of a busy street and the noise of traffic. If your puppy is frightened, do not force him to confront whatever is frightening him. Give your puppy a chance to watch what is going on while you give lots of praise and reassurance, and you will find that, in most cases, your puppy's natural curiosity will win the day!

## LEAD-TRAINING

If you have bought a puppy with the intention of showing him, never leave a collar on all the time. It will make the hair around the neck flatter, and this does not help the dog to present a clean outline in the ring. However, a collar is a must for a pet dog.

You need to get your puppy used to the feel of a collar. Start off with a soft collar, so that he hardly knows he is wearing it. You can buy an adjustable collar, which will fit your puppy while he is growing.

- As soon as your puppy accepts the collar, you can attach the lead.
- To begin with, just allow your puppy to walk around the living room, and follow where the puppy chooses to go.
- If all goes well, you can proceed to walk up and down the garden path, encouraging your puppy to follow you.
- It is a good idea to have a biscuit or a ball in your hand, and, if the pup protests or puts on the brakes, entice him to walk towards you.
- Play with him with the lead on, and, as he grows older, make him walk beside you, usually on your left-hand side.
- When he pulls, pull him back and give the command "Heel".
- If you start your lead-training at about 10 weeks, your puppy should be ready to walk on the road as soon as the inoculation programme is completed.
- Do not allow children to take a puppy out alone on the road. A quick pull from the puppy can catch a child unawares, and this could end in disaster.

*Above: Use a treat or a toy to encourage your pup to walk on a lea*

*Below: Practice at home has paid of,*

## BASIC COMMANDS

Do not make the mistake of thinking that you cannot train your puppy until he is six months old.

A puppy as young as eight weeks old is very receptive, and there is no reason why you should not introduce basic commands, building up to basic Obedience exercises.

### SHORT AND SWEET!

It is important to remember that your puppy is still very young, and his concentration span will be very limited. Keep your 'lessons' very short, giving plenty of praise, and always end on a good note. If your puppy is enjoying himself, he is far more likely to respond to your wishes. If you feel tired or short-tempered, do not attempt to train your puppy on that day. Lessons should be fun – you will achieve nothing if you find yourself getting cross or frustrated. If your puppy fails to understand what is required, go back to an exercise you know he can do. In this way, you will end your training session positively, rather than with a sense of failure. The next time you train, go back to the 'difficult' exercise, and you will almost certainly make progress.

## TEACHING THE SIT

This is an easy command to teach, and it will be useful throughout your dog's life. A good time to teach your puppy to sit is at mealtimes. As you offer the puppy his meal, give the command "Sit", place your hand on your puppy's hindquarters and exert slight pressure. In no time, your puppy will sit every time a meal is offered, and he will also have learned the command.

Alternatively, show him a treat in your hand, and when he follows it with his nose, put it just above his head, so he has to put his bottom on the floor to reach it. Say "Sit" when he sits, and give lots of praise and a treat.

*Hold a treat above your puppy's head to encourage him to sit.*

## TEACHING THE DOWN

This is a straightforward exercise, but it could be a life-saver if your dog learns to respond instantly to the command "Down", no matter what the situation.

Your tone of voice is important when giving this command; it is important to use a deep, firm voice, as this aids the puppy's understanding.

Start with your puppy in the Sit position, and give the command

"Down", while showing him a treat that you are holding on the floor. The puppy will try to get the treat, but only release it when his tummy is on the ground. Then, say "Down", praise him, and give him the treat.

*Lower a treat towards the floor and your puppy will follow it, going into the Down position.*

## TEACHING THE STAY

This exercise should be built up gradually – there is no point in being ambitious before your puppy understands what is required – you will just end up with a thoroughly confused dog.

- To start with, keep your puppy on a lead, and give the command "Sit".
- Then, back away from your puppy, just to the end of the lead, and give the command "Stay", using the

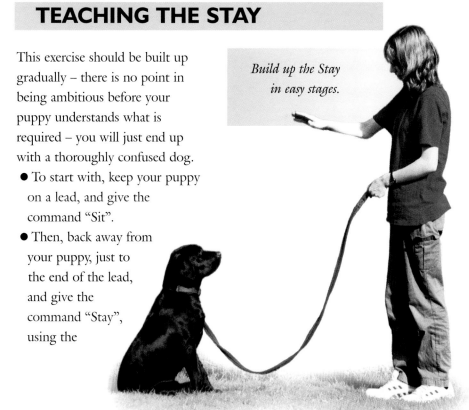

*Build up the Stay in easy stages.*

appropriate hand signal – hand held upwards, palm facing towards the puppy.

- When the exercise is finished, return to your puppy's side and give plenty of praise.

- When you are confident that your puppy understands what is required, you can gradually increase the distance between you, and, eventually, leave your puppy without a lead.

*Crouch down to your puppy's level and call him to you.*

Your puppy will learn the command "Come" in the first few days. Just call your puppy by his name, and add the command, "Rover, Come".

Encourage your puppy to come to you by crouching down to his level with your arms outstretched. This exercise can be developed as the puppy grows older, in conjunction with the Stay exercise,

## TEACHING RECALL

until you complete a proper recall. However, do not be tempted to rush basic training.

- Start with your Labrador puppy on the lead, on your left-hand side, and give the command "Sit".

- Then, give the command "Wait", and back away from your puppy, giving the hand signal you use in the Stay exercise with your palm facing your dog.
- Eventually, you will be able to turn and walk away from your puppy, but this should only be introduced when you are confident that your puppy will stay in position.
- When you are ready, stop, repeat the command "Wait", reinforcing this with the appropriate hand signal.

- Wait a couple of seconds and call in your puppy – "Rover, Come", opening your arms to welcome him to you.
- Reward him with lots of praise.
- Do not confuse your puppy by calling him to you when you have given the command "Stay".

The Stay exercise and the Recall exercise should be separated in your dog's mind, and so it is easier to use a different command, i.e. "Wait", when you are doing a Recall.

*As your pup progresses, you can work on a formal recall exercise.*

## TRAINING TARGETS

By the time your Labrador is six months old, you will hopefully have a reasonably well-behaved dog, who is pretty reliable. Your puppy is house-trained, lead-trained, and comes when he is called. He may even sit and stay on command.

You will have discovered by this time that the only way to teach your dog anything is by repetition. Repeat a lesson over and over again until your pup has absorbed it, and do not go on to the next lesson until you are satisfied that this is so.

### Basic Instincts

Have patience (loads of it!), and be very liberal with your praise. Above all, the training sessions must be fun for the pup. If you get bogged down, and tempers get frayed, training takes twice as long, and you are unlikely to achieve such good results.

The Labrador Retriever is one of the gundog or sporting breeds,

*Make training sessions fun, so your Labrador enjoys working with you.*

and the basic instincts to retrieve and to please are there in your puppy, waiting for you to further his education. This is an intelligent breed, and your Labrador is likely to become bored if he is left completely to his own devices.

# 5 TRAINING CHALLENGES

The type of training you give your dog depends on what you want to achieve.

You may be content with a well-behaved family companion, or you may be more competitive and want to try your hand at Obedience or Agility competitions.

Equally, you may have bought your puppy to be a shooting companion, or you may want to compete in Working Tests and have dreams of running in Field Trials.

Whatever area you decide to get involved with, make sure you go to a good training club run by people who are well qualified in their field.

There are also many excellent books on gundog and Obedience training, and these are written by

experts with a proven track record on their subject. In the scope of this book, I will merely outline the essentials of what is required, and hope that you go on to pursue your new hobby in more depth.

## OBEDIENCE TRAINING

All dogs should be taught basic obedience, and many owners are quite happy when their dog masters the basics. However, some owners are more competitive and the dogs certainly seem to enjoy the stimulation of responding to increasingly complex commands. The Labrador is certainly intelligent enough, and there is no reason why your dog cannot do well in this field.

It is important to start when your pup is about six months of age, and you cannot expect to join in more advanced Obedience classes until your dog is walking on a lead, sitting, or perhaps sitting and staying, and

*The Labrador is a natural retriever, so he will soon learn to pick up a dumb-bell.*

coming when called.

Many training clubs run puppy classes, and these will help you to teach your pup the basics. This is done in the company of other pups, and so it is an excellent way of teaching your dog to concentrate despite distractions. These classes are usually run weekly, some twice-weekly, depending on availability of the venue or trainer, and they will expect you to continue training on your own at home.

As with retrieving classes, the instructor is always someone who is qualified in this branch of dog training and has the ability to teach others.

*In competition, the dog must present the dumb-bell to his handler.*

Nine times out of ten, it is the owner who needs the training, and Obedience trainers do seem to have the knack of training both dog and owner.

One word of advice – if you intend to show your dog, mention this to the trainer, and the Stand exercise will probably be substituted for the Sit exercise

*The obedience-trained Lab will learn to stay with the handler out of sight.*

51

when you come to a halt. This is because sitting in the show ring would be a positive disadvantage, when the aim is to get your dog to pose in order to show himself off to full advantage. Some dog shows have Obedience trials, and the dogs entered in these need not be entered for the show.

There is a set programme for each test, and a judge calculates the points to be awarded. There are also shows for Obedience dogs only.

## OBEDIENCE TITLES

If you get really hooked on competitive Obedience, there are plenty of titles to be won. In the UK, these include Companion Dog (CD), Utility Dog (UD), and Tracking Dog (TD), in ascending order of difficulty. In North America, the corresponding titles are: Companion Dog (CD), Companion Dog Excellent (CDX), Utility Dog (UD), Utility Dog Excellent (UDX), Tracking Dog (TD), and Tracking Dog Excellent (TDX).

# AGILITY TRAINING

Agility is an increasingly popular activity, and both owners and dogs get a lot of fun from it. Obviously, the Labrador is not as fast as some breeds, such as the Border Collie, but accuracy is also important, and the Labrador will have no trouble negotiating the obstacles.

It is essential that you do not attempt to train your Labrador for Agility until he is at least 12 months of age. The exertion involved in this sport could prove hazardous to a growing puppy.

However, while you are waiting to enrol at an Agility training club, the time can be usefully

*Most Labradors enjoy the challenge of Agility.*

## TACKLING OBSTACLES

The apparatus for Agility competitions includes an A-frame, a dog walk, a see-saw, hurdles, a tunnel, a tyre, and weaving poles. Many newcomers think their dog will be frightened by the tunnel, but, for some reason, nearly all dogs love running through this piece of equipment. The weaving poles pose the greatest challenge, particularly for the bigger dogs. With this exercise, there is no substitute for practice.

spent working on basic obedience. Your dog will be working off-lead, and, therefore, you must have complete control over him. The obstacles must be tackled when you give the command, and the dog must not leap off before he has negotiated the obstacle correctly. Instant response to the commands of "Wait" and "Down" are essential.

It is also important to have built up a good relationship with your Labrador, as you are asking him to attempt tasks that are well

*The tyre (above) and the weaves (below) are among the more difficult obstacles.*

*Despite the steeepness of the A-frame, most dogs take to it readily.*

outside his normal compass. However, once the dogs are familiar with the obstacles, they thoroughly enjoy the challenge of tackling them – and, in most cases, the hardest job is to slow down the dog so that he listens to instructions. The Agility course is tackled against the clock, and time is lost for faults along the way round. Both dogs and handlers have to be fit to be successful in this activity.

Even if you reach the highest level of competition, this is a marvellous way of channelling your dog's energies, and building up a good working relationship.

## CONTACT POINTS

When a dog is negotiating the A-frame, the dog walk and the see-saw, he must hit the 'contact points' going on or off the equipment. You will need to teach a command such as "Wait" or "Touch" so that your dog hits the correct area.

## GUN TRAINING

If you decide that you want to gun train your puppy, it is a good idea to join your local Labrador or gundog club. These clubs run gundog training days, usually supervised by someone who has great knowledge and understanding of both dogs and novice handlers. Training in this atmosphere enables your dog to get accustomed to working in the company of other dogs and to the various distractions he might not otherwise encounter if he was trained on his own.

Most clubs have access to land of varying types – plough, scrubland, woods and water – you do not have to own a country estate to train your gundog! I know of quite a few people who, when they started gun training, lived in town with a postage-stamp-sized garden, a park nearby, and just the monthly visit to the training classes, and they have become well known and successful in the Field Trial world.

*The Labrador is born to retrieve – on land and in water.*

Dogs must be taught to stop on the whistle, and also to come (quickly) on the same whistle. In the novice class, all the other dogs and owners will be just like yourself, so there is no need to worry that you are going to make complete fools of yourselves. There is always a great deal of good-natured rivalry and leg-pulling at these sorts of gatherings.

When you watch the advanced dogs doing all sort of clever things with double dummies and unseen retrieves, just remember – they also started in the novice class.

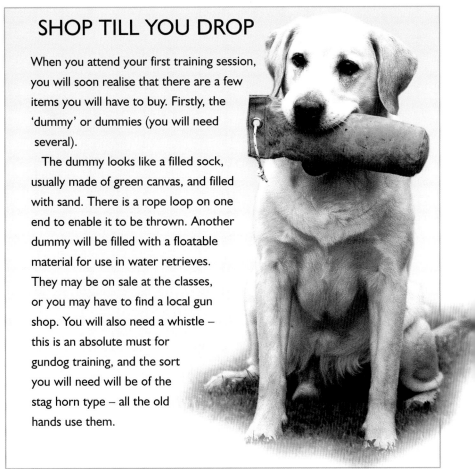

## SHOP TILL YOU DROP

When you attend your first training session, you will soon realise that there are a few items you will have to buy. Firstly, the 'dummy' or dummies (you will need several).

The dummy looks like a filled sock, usually made of green canvas, and filled with sand. There is a rope loop on one end to enable it to be thrown. Another dummy will be filled with a floatable material for use in water retrieves. They may be on sale at the classes, or you may have to find a local gun shop. You will also need a whistle – this is an absolute must for gundog training, and the sort you will need will be of the stag horn type – all the old hands use them.

# RETRIEVING

We always started our pups retrieving at home, just to ensure that they do retrieve. There is nothing more embarrassing than standing in line for your first retrieve, watching the dummy land in full view and not too far away, giving the command to your pup, and then wishing the ground would open up and swallow you as he yawns, scratches and rolls over on his back!

## Off The Lead

A long passage-way is an ideal place for training pups. The dog runs straight out and straight back with the dummy – there is nowhere else to go. Make sure you have lots of tidbits, and always give plenty of praise when the dog returns with the dummy. The simple procedure certainly beats chasing your puppy over a 40-acre field in order to get back the dummy! At the training class, your pup should now be walking at heel on and off the lead. At this stage, the line of handlers and their dogs move off, and, at a command, they stop. A dummy will be thrown for you, and, when you are instructed, you will send in the pup to retrieve it.

If your Labrador comes straight

*Start by using a toy to encourage the retrieve.*

back to you, make him sit still, holding the dummy, and gently take it from him. Then give plenty of praise.

Naturally, this exercise will be repeated many times until the pup is going further out for his retrieves.

You will gradually proceed from here until your dog is retrieving 'unseen' dummies, doing double dummies, retrieving from water, obeying hand signals, getting used to gunfire, and, eventually, picking up cold game (birds shot earlier and kept frozen until needed).

*In time, your Labrador will become a polished performer.*

## FIELD TRIALS

Competing in Field Trials is another thing entirely from keeping and training a shooting companion. In fact, I believe that Field Trialling has become so specialised, you should really purchase your pup from a kennel that has a reputation for producing this type of dog. Take advice from Field Trial trainers. Speed, an instant response to commands, and a highly developed scenting ability are absolute musts in this highly competitive sport.

## THE VERSATILE RETRIEVER

Although, first and foremost, the Labrador Retriever is a gundog, the breed's outstanding temperament, intelligence and trainability have led to other uses being evolved for him over the years.

### GUIDE DOGS

Labradors are used as guide dogs for the blind worldwide. In the early days of the charity, German Shepherd Dogs were used, and, although they are still employed in this role, Labradors and Labrador-crosses are now used most extensively for guide dog work. Many Labrador breeders have provided guide dogs over the

*The Labrador is well-suited to guide dog work.*

*Guide dog puppies are given an intensive programme of socialisation.*

years, although now the Guide Dogs for the Blind Association in Britain runs its own breeding programme, which is tailormade to produce the type of dog that is most suitable for guide dog work.

The success of the Association's breeding programme is reflected in the pass rate that is achieved in the litters – nearly always over 70 per cent and sometimes up to 100 per cent. Kennels are of a very high standard, and the kennel staff are given a superb grounding in kennel management and

These are the reasons why the Labrador suits guide dog work so well:

● The breed is medium-sized.
● It has a low-maintenance coat, which a blind person can care for without undue difficulty.
● The Lab is intelligent, willing to please, and easy to train.
● The typical temperament is sound and steady.
● The Lab is loyal and affectionate.

further. One day, the dog will be responsible for a blind person's life, so he must be 100 per cent trustworthy in all circumstances he may encounter.

Having passed the initial test, which is usually when the puppy is nine to 12 months old age, the trainee guide dog is now ready to go to work.

## Final Step

He is placed with a guide dog trainer who, among other things, teaches the use of the harness, the correct procedure for crossing the road, avoiding obstacles and generally how to guide a blind person in a busy, urban environment.

The final step is matching the dog to a blind person, and then dog and owner undergo a period of intensive training.

After qualifying, specialised

puppy/dog handling.

Puppies are taken into the homes of puppy walkers, and here they learn the basics of obedience and are exposed to as many different situations as possible. It costs a great deal of money to train each dog to the exacting standard required, so, if a dog does not come up to scratch as far as temperament and reliability is concerned at this early age, there is no point in proceeding any staff provide continued care with a series of home visits to ensure that the new partnership is working well.

A guide dog works hard, and, although in most cases he has a very enjoyable off-duty life, a working guide dog will usually retire at the age of eight or nine.

These dogs are often re-homed with friends or relatives of the blind owner, or with members of the public who are willing to take on an older dog.

## HEARING DOGS FOR THE DEAF

**This is a relatively new role for dogs, and, again, the Labrador has adapted well to the work. The dogs are trained to alert their owner and then to run towards the sound of a noise, e.g. when the telephone or doorbell rings, or when the timer on the cooker goes off.**

*The biddable Labrador adapts well to the role of hearing dog.*

HEARING DOG FOR THE DEAF

# DOGS FOR THE DISABLED

This is a relatively new way of using dogs, and it has been found that trainee guide dogs who failed to make the grade can be used in this capacity, following extra specialised training.

These dogs do an invaluable job in helping their owners around the house, opening doors, picking up the telephone receiver, switching lights on and off, taking the milk bottles outside, and fetching articles that are required.

I have seen one emptying clothes from a tumble-drier, pulling them out gently with his teeth and putting them into a laundry basket.

*A dog for the disabled makes everyday life easier for his owner.*

# THERAPY DOGS

Therapy dogs do a marvellous job, visiting hospitals, residential homes for the elderly, and schools. Labradors are used extensively for this work, as their friendly, outgoing temperament is ideal.

Many a child has got over a fear of dogs because a Labrador has visited the school, where he has stood patiently and allowed the children to pat him or even to walk him a short way on his lead.

This is an ideal way of teaching children how to behave with a dog.

In a hospital ward, a Labrador seems to be just the right height for a patient to be able to pat his head without too much effort, and this communication has proved to be of tremendous therapeutic value.

In residential homes for the elderly, a visit from a dog is eagerly awaited, and provides a great talking point.

*Sweet-natured and affectionate, the Labrador is an ideal therapy dog.*

# POLICE
# AND SNIFFER DOGS

The German Shepherd Dog is the most commonly used
police dog, but Labradors are also used a great deal. They are
trained in most aspects of police work – tracking, guarding, and
latterly as sniffer dogs, to hunt out drugs and explosives. Because of its
high degree of intelligence as a breed, a Labrador can be trained to be
aggressive on command. This is a reversal of the usual temperament of the
breed, but apparently, it is a lesson that, once learned, they excel at. The
favoured colour for this work is black, although all three colours are used.
Training dogs for use as sniffer dogs for drugs and explosives started in
the 1960s. Many breeds were tested, and, at that time, Labradors
topped the poll, although Springer Spaniels are now very popular.
The Spaniels are smaller, and, as they often have to be lifted
up and put through windows or into loft spaces, you
can see why the Springer wins
over an 80lb Labrador!

# 6 HEALTH CARE

The Labrador Retriever is an active, healthy breed that is easy to care for, and, hopefully, visits to the vet will be few and far between.

However, all dogs are likely to suffer from an ailment or minor accident at some point in their lives, and it is advisable to acquire some knowledge so that you can assess your dog's condition and administer basic treatments.

## FINDING A VET

The vet is a key figure in your dog's life, and it is important you find a vet that you can feel at ease with. You want someone who will take the time to explain everything to you: what is wrong with your dog, the type of medication prescribed, possible side effects, and roughly how long the condition will take to clear up.

It is also important to watch how the vet gets on with your Labrador.

The golden rule when caring for your Labrador is, if in doubt, call your vet. If a dog is taken to the vet in the early stages of an illness, this can not only save the dog from suffering a lot of discomfort, it can also save you a lot of worry.

## GET KITTED UP FOR FIRST AID

There are a number of minor ailments or injuries that you can cope with in the home, and it is advisable to have a small first-aid kit, so you are equipped to deal with the more common problems.

I suggest you keep in stock:
- Cotton wool (cotton)
- Bandages (crepe and cotton)
- A roll of inch-wide adhesive tape (for fastening a bandage)
- A mild disinfectant (suitable for washing cuts)
- Ear drops
- A box of cotton buds
- A bottle of hydrogen peroxide (for the treatment of eczema)
- A bottle of liquid paraffin (for the treatment of constipation)
- A treatment for diarrhoea (ask your vet for advice)
- A thermometer
- A bottle of cough medicine
- Antiseptic powder
- Antiseptic cream
- A pair of scissors
- A pair of tweezers.

## COMMON PROBLEMS

### COUGHS

Coughs can have many causes. The most distressing and contagious is kennel cough, which can be caught by all dogs, not just those that are confined to kennels. The signs are an exceptionally dry, husky cough, which is very distressing.

This is a contagious disease that has to take its course, and all you can do is relieve the symptoms with the treatment prescribed by your vet.

It is essential that you keep your dog at home and avoid all contact with other dogs until you are confident that your Labrador has completely recovered.

There is a vaccination against kennel cough, which is quite effective. This is not a life-threatening condition, but old dogs and puppies are obviously more at risk.

Coughing can also be a sign of worm infestation, and, in rare cases, it may be the first sign of heart disease. If your dog is getting on in years and is coughing, you would be wise to ask your vet for advice.

*Regular exercise is an essential part of preventative health care.*

## CUTS

Minor cuts should be cleaned with antiseptic and then left to heal. Dogs usually lick a wound clean, and, provided the dog does not keep on licking to excess, this usually helps the cut to heal.

If the cut is more serious, it may be better to cover it with a bandage, providing the cut is located on a part of the body that can be easily bandaged. Make sure the bandage is not too tight, and remember to fasten it with adhesive tape, and not a safety-pin.

If your dog has a really deep cut, stitches will probably be required. You will need to put a temporary bandage on the wound, and then go to the vet as soon as possible, first telephoning so that he or she knows what to expect. If the vet decides to come to your house, try to keep the dog as quiet as possible, and, if you can, hold the edges of the cut together.

After the wound has been stitched, it is important to make sure that the dog does not worry at the stitches. If this happens, the vet may suggest that your dog wears a plastic collar – sometimes known as an Elizabethan collar.

*The energetic Labrador can get himself into mischief.*

*Your Labrador's ears are a potential source of trouble.*

Ears need checking regularly in order to keep them clean and sweet-smelling. When ears get dirty and wax builds up, they can be prone to infection.

If your Labrador keeps shaking his head, or one ear hangs down lower than the other, there is probably a problem.

Labradors love swimming, but, when your dog comes out of the water, make sure you dry his ears. You only need to dry the external part of the ear – never poke anything inside it.

# TAKE GOOD CARE OF THE EARS

Sometimes, you will find a black deposit in the ears, which could be caused by ear mites. Use a few drops of an ear cleaner, drop them into the ear and gently massage it. Leave for a few seconds and then wipe away any deposit from the outer ear with a cotton bud or cotton wool. If, after a few days of treatment, the dog is still uncomfortable, then take him to the vet.

## DEALING WITH ECZEMA

This starts with a wet patch on the skin, usually as a result of the dog getting overheated or suffering an allergic reaction. It can also be caused by fleas. Cut the hair from around the affected area, and dab either with hydrogen peroxide or an antiseptic solution. The wet patch should soon dry up without spreading any further, and the hair will slowly grow over. If the wet patch persists, ask your vet for advice.

## IF THE EYES HAVE IT

If your Labrador gets runny eyes, especially in the summer, this can be caused by dust. Some dogs also suffer from a form of hay-fever. Bathing the eyes with cold tea (no milk or sugar!) or a proprietary eye-wash, will remedy this. If your dog has matter in the eyes, or constantly runny eyes that seem irritated, ask your vet for advice.

This could be a symptom of a more serious problem, particularly if your dog appears to be off-colour, so professional advice should be sought.

Constantly running eyes can be caused by a condition called entropion. The eyelid rolls inward and the eyelashes come into

*If you have any concerns about your dog's eyes, do not delay in seeking expert advice.*

contact with the eye-ball. In severe cases, it can cause blindness, but it can be treated by a simple operation. As this can be a hereditary defect, the dog should not be used for breeding.

## GETTING RID OF FLEAS

**Some dogs are allergic to fleas, and will keep on worrying and scratching at the flea bites. The trick is to stop this before the bites turn into eczema. The best treatments are available from your vet, and include sprays, spot-on treatments (where just a few spots of insecticide are applied to the back of the neck), flea birth control, and powders. Remember, your home, car and furnishings need treating too!**

# LAMENESS

There can be many reasons for a dog becoming lame, but it is always worth checking the feet to start with. It could well be that a thorn or a sharp stone has got stuck in the pad. This is where your tweezers come in handy. After removing the foreign object, dab the affected spot with a little antiseptic, and there should be no further problems.

Sometimes, a dog will cut his pad and a stitch may be required, or he may break a nail. In both these cases, make sure you keep the wound site clean, and keep a close check until it has healed.

If you can find nothing wrong with the feet and your dog is still lame, it could mean that he has a sprain. Feel for any heat in the leg, and then bathe in alternate warm and cold water. Try to make the dog rest as much as possible. If the lameness persists, consult your vet.

*Get into the habit of checking your dog's feet after walks.*

# STOMACH UPSETS

If you suspect your Labrador has swallowed something that is likely to disagree with him, such as a handkerchief, a sock, or a small stone, a dose of liquid paraffin will help the article to work its way through. You can give two or three doses, but, if you get no results or if your dog goes off his food or looks bloated, and if he is visibly distressed, you will need professional advice.

I have recovered two nylon slip leads, a handkerchief and a linen table napkin using this method! It is also a useful remedy if your dog appears to be suffering from constipation. If, on the other hand, your dog has diarrhoea, you will need to starve your dog for 24 hours. Make sure there is plenty of clean drinking water available at all times, as it is important that the dog does not become dehydrated.

Diarrhoea is a condition that must not be ignored, and, if it goes on for a day or two without signs of improvement, call your vet. If you see blood in the motions, you should contact your vet immediately.

*An inquisitive pup may swallow something which could prove hazardous.*

There are many reasons why a dog may develop a temperature, and, if your dog is off-colour, it may be useful to take his temperature to help to assess the overall condition.

- Insert a thermometer 1½ inches (2½ to 4cms) into the dog's anal canal, using a twisting motion. This can be facilitated if you apply a little petroleum jelly to the end of the thermometer.

## TAKING THE TEMPERATURE

- Hold it in place for two to three minutes, making sure you keep the dog steady, and then gently withdraw it.
- The average temperature for an adult dog is 101.5 degrees Fahrenheit (38.5 degrees Celsius).

# WORMS

## ROUNDWORM

This is the most common type of worm, and most dogs will have an infestation at some point in their lives, particularly in their first year. When you buy your puppy, he should have been treated for roundworm, and you should be given details of the worming programme, and when the next treatment is due. Your vet will tell you how often you need to worm (it is usually three to four times a year according to the treatment used).

If you suspect that your dog has worms, the signs to look for are:
- A loss of condition
- A dry, 'starey' coat (i.e. the coat does not lie down in a sleek fashion; it stands up slightly from the skin and it lacks the gloss that a good coat should have)
- Bad breath
- A voracious appetite (although a loss of appetite can also indicate worms)
- A pot-belly.
Worming tablets can be bought

from your vet. Use as directed, and do not be tempted to 'throw in an extra one for luck', as this could do more harm than good. Some worming preparations will actually melt the worms and you will see no signs of them in the dog's motions; others will dislodge the worms and they will be seen when expelled.

## TAPEWORM

If you live and exercise your dog in sheep country, you run the risk of your dog contracting tapeworms, especially if you run your dog over sheep pastures. Even the most well-raised dog seems unable to resist eating sheep droppings from time to time, and this results in tapeworm infestation.

Tapeworms are a little more difficult to dislodge than roundworms, because they actually hook themselves on to the intestine and grow from there. They are a segmented parasite, and segments tend to break off, very often remaining around the dog's anus. If you see small, square-looking segments in that area, accompanied by poor condition, bad breath, etc., seek veterinary advice.

*Routine worming should form part of your care programme.*

*If you are worried about your Labrador's condition, seek veterinary advice.*

# HEREDITARY DISEASES

Like most other breeds, the Labrador Retriever does have a few hereditary diseases. It is important to be aware of these before buying a puppy, so you can check with the breeder about the health of their lines, and ask to see the relevant documentation (e.g. hip-score certificates).

## PROGRESSIVE RENAL ATROPHY (PRA)

All responsible breeders have their breeding stock checked annually by an authorised vet for this disease. As the name implies, it is an atrophying of the retina. This can take quite a while to develop, and some dogs may be seven years old or even older before the condition becomes apparent to the owner, although it may also appear at an earlier age.

If you plan to use your dog for breeding, it is advisable to have the eyes checked as soon as the

> *Dogs used for breeding must be tested clear of inherited diseases.*

dog is old enough (i.e. 12 months), and then on an annual basis thereafter. This condition results in blindness, and so all preventative measures must be taken to reduce its incidence.

## HIP DYSPLASIA

This condition affects the ball and socket joint of the hind legs, and it is more likely to appear in the larger and heavier breeds. A dog can be born with seemingly normal hips, and it is only when he matures that the problem becomes apparent.

The only way to detect hip dysplasia is by X-ray, and the earliest age that you can have your dog tested is 12 months (24 months in the US), and the results are then scored. The degree of hip dysplasia can vary widely, and some dysplastic dogs are never lame in their lifetime. However, responsible breeders try

to breed from relatively sound stock, and, in this way, the number of dogs suffering from this condition is greatly reduced. Dogs suffering from severe hip dysplasia can undergo surgery.

## OSTEOCHONDROSIS

There is evidence to suggest that this is an inherited condition, although other factors, such as injury, excessive exercise and oversupplementation of additives to the diet are contributing factors. It usually occurs in the larger, fast-growing breeds, and develops between four and 12 months of age.

The problem occurs when cartilage flakes off from the bones, and this may occur in the shoulder, hocks or stifles, causing gradual lameness.

Rest may solve the problem, but surgery is the only solution in more severe cases. This is most successful when it is the shoulder that is affected.

*Be especially careful to monitor exercise during the vulnerable growing period.*

## SUMMARY

**We are fortunate that the Labrador is a hardy, no-nonsense breed, and most dogs will enjoy a long, happy and healthy life. Make sure you keep up with a preventative health care programme, and monitor diet and exercise, and you will be rewarded with many years of trouble-free companionship.**

## ABOUT THE AUTHOR

Diana Beckett has owned Labradors since her early teens, and she has bred and exhibited the breed for the last 35 years. She managed a large show kennel in America for several years, and, during this time, she made up 15 American Champions. She has made up four home-bred Champions, as well as having Champions in Germany and Denmark. Her stock is well known in the show ring, and in working kennels.

Diana is an international Championship show judge, and she has been to the USA, Sweden, Finland, Denmark, Holland, France and Germany on judging appointments.

In 1990, she judged the breed at Crufts.